BIBLICALLY

Based Coloring & Activity Book For Fall

WELCOME

Thank you for your purchase of the Biblically Based Coloring & Activity Book for Fall.

INSIDE THIS BOOK YOU'LL FIND

- Coloring Pages (many with scripture)
- Educational Activity Pages
- Writing Prompts
- Gratitude Journal for kids

We pray that your family will find this book to be both fun and faith building.

Spirit of **TRUTH**

A podcast by Melissa Collins

FALL FEASTS

Fall is my favorite time of year. The weather is cool and enjoyable to be outside. It is also the time when Americans celebrate Thanksgiving. Thanksgiving is a wonderful holiday when family and friends gather to show thanks or gratitude to God for all their blessings.

DID YOU KNOW?

The Bible also has a list of holy days, or what we would call holidays, that God asks us to celebrate or observe.

Three of these seven celebrations are held in the fall.

- The Feast of Trumpets
- The Day of Atonement
- The Feast of Tabernacles

FOR MORE INFO SEE LEVITICUS 23

WHAT IS GRATITUDE?

Gratitude is the expression of appreciation for what one has. Practicing gratitude means making conscious efforts to count one's blessings and notice the goodness in life.

BEING GRATEFUL...

- keeps you calm and joyful
- boosts mood and self-esteem
- reduces feelings of loneliness and isolation
- helps develop stronger relationships
- improves quality of sleep
- encourages positivity and optimism
- makes life more enjoyable

> **GIVE THANKS IN ALL CIRCUMSTANCES; FOR THIS IS GOD'S WILL FOR YOU IN CHRIST JESUS.**
> 1 Thessalonians 5:18

In Hebrew, the word "hodu" means both Thanksgiving and turkey!

Through the middle of the street of the city; also, on either side of the river, the tree of life with its twelve kinds of fruit, yielding its fruit each month. The leaves of the tree were for the healing of the nations.
Revelation 22:2

DRAW 3 THINGS YOU'RE GRATEFUL FOR TODAY

Name: date:

Autumn Leaves Matching

Connect the leaves with their mirror image.

FALL SEASON

Find the differences between two pictures.

Dear

I am thankful to have you in my life because...

From

Grateful!

Fall objects

Color and cut out the objects from the bottom of the page, then paste them where correspond.

O give thanks unto the LORD, for he is good: for his mercy endureth for ever. Psalm 107:1

Pumpkin Patch I Spy

Explore the pumpkin patch and find each of the items listed. Mark off each item when you find it and then describe it to another person using the sentence below.

A(n) _____ is a type of _____ that _____ .

- ○ acorn
- ○ apple
- ○ barn
- ○ cider
- ○ corn
- ○ cornucopia
- ○ hay
- ○ jack-o'-lantern
- ○ jam

- ○ pie
- ○ pitchfork
- ○ pumpkin
- ○ rake
- ○ scarecrow
- ○ sunflower
- ○ tractor
- ○ turkey
- ○ wildflowers

Therefore the Lord blessed the Sabbath day and made it holy. Exodus 20:11

Name:_____   Date:_____

Gratitude Journal for students

Instruction: Take a moment to think about what are you grateful for today. Write down your thoughts.

> List three things you're grateful for today.

> Describe a small act of kindness you witnessed or received.

FALL SEASON

Draw and color the other halves of the pictures below.

 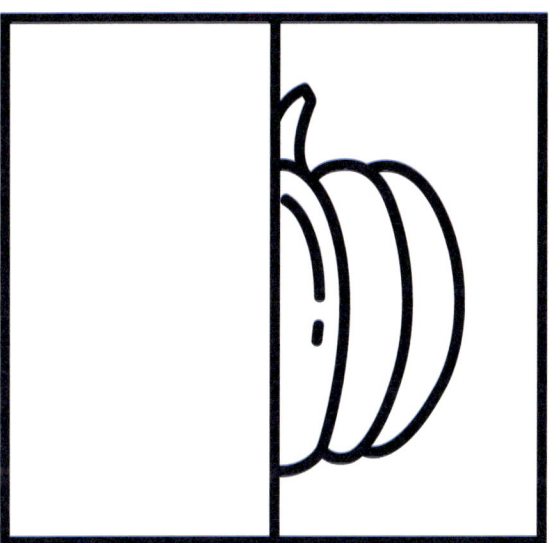

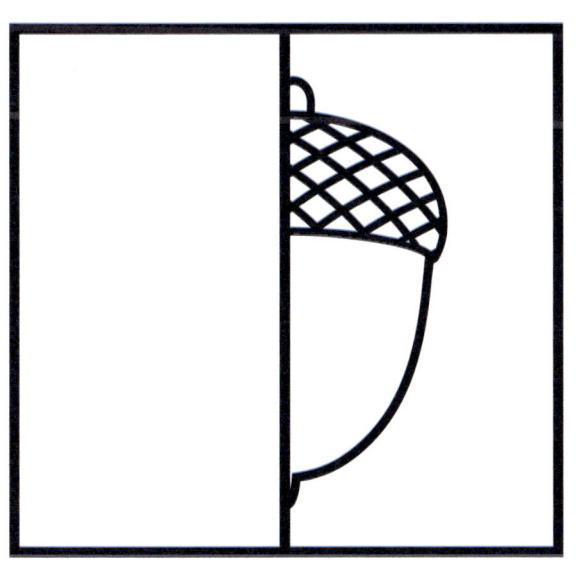 

And Joseph gathered corn as the sand of the sea, very much, until he left numbering; for it was without number. Genesis 41:48-54

PUMPKIN COUNTING

the students found many pumpkins at the pumpkin patch. Color the pumpkins in each column and then write the number of pumpkins in each column in the space provided. When finished color the pumpkins on the reverse and practice your handwriting.

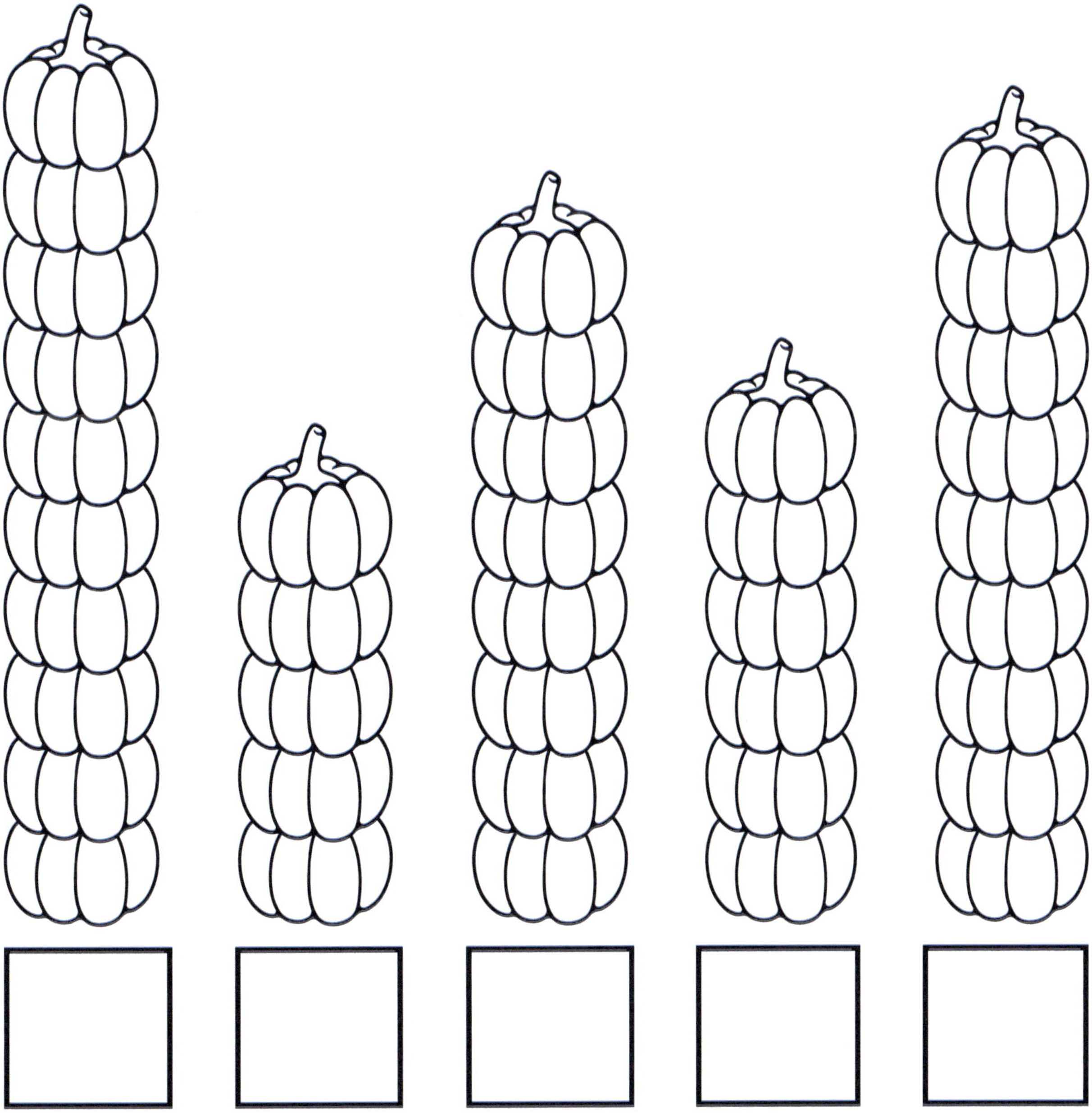

then I will send rain on your land in its season, both autumn and spring rains, so that you may gather in your grain, new wine and olive oil. Deut 11:14

Name_____

I AM THANKFUL FOR

Write down one thing that you are thankful for starting with each letter.

T _____

H _____

A _____

N _____

K _____

F _____

U _____

L _____

Likewise, every good tree bears good fruit, but a bad tree bears bad fruit.
Matthew 7:17

Find the Differences - Fall

Can you find the 5 differences in these two pictures?

Name   Date

THANKFUL PIE

Draw or write something you are thankful for in each slice of pie.

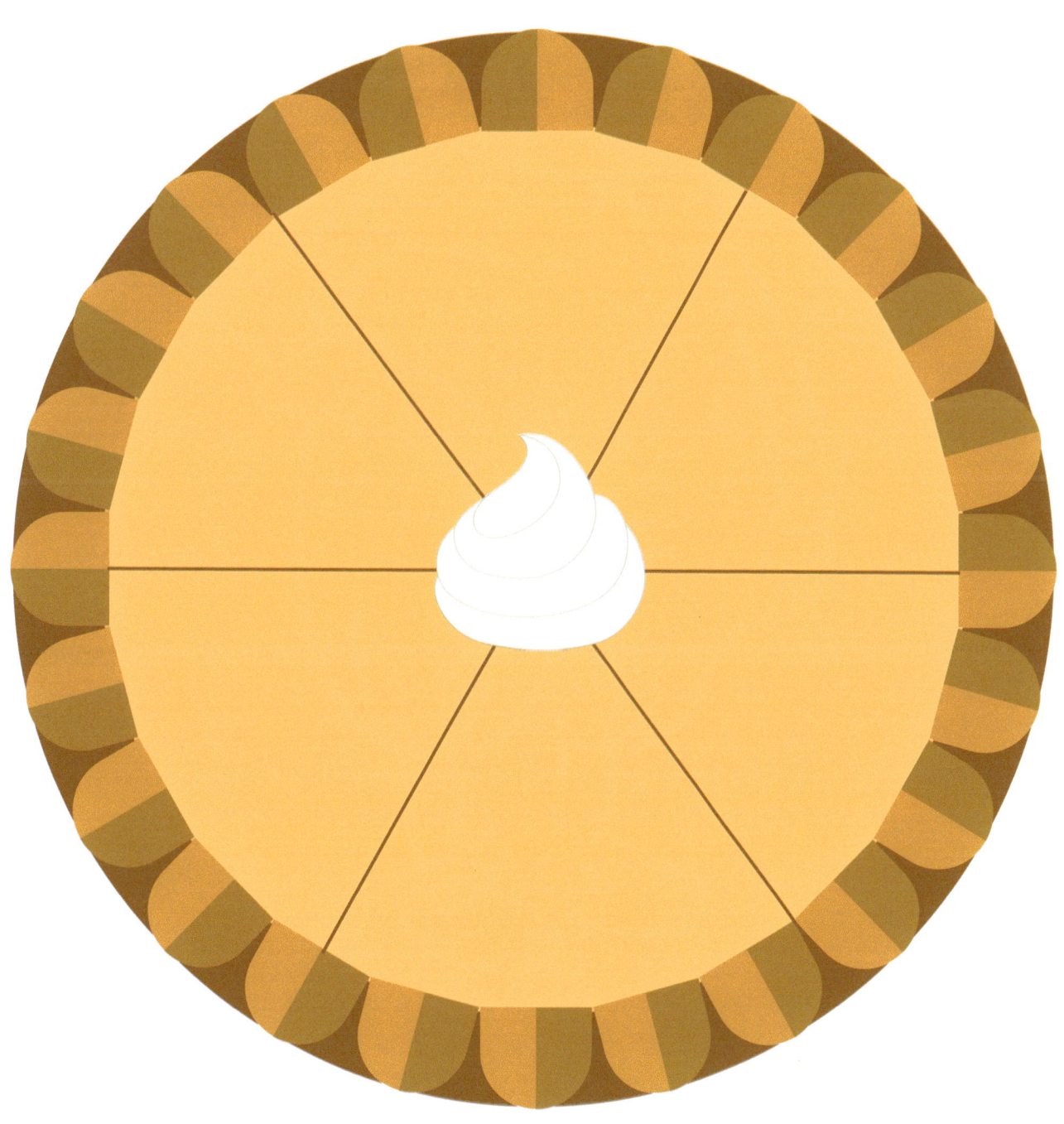

Name: _____ Score: _____

Numbers 1 - 25

Fill in the missing numbers.

Give thanks to the Lord, for he is good. His love endures forever.
Psalms 136:1

THANKSGIVING
FAVORITE FOOD

Write about your favorite Thanksgiving recipe and draw its picture below.

My favorite dish

"Celebrate the Festival of Harvest with the firstfruits of the crops you sow in your field. "Celebrate the Festival of Ingathering at the end of the year, when you gather in your crops from the field. Exodus 23:16

Name: _____ Date: _____

AUTUMN-THEMED FINISH THE PICTURE

Draw the other halves and color the pictures.
Then, trace the words.

leaf

acorn

pumpkin

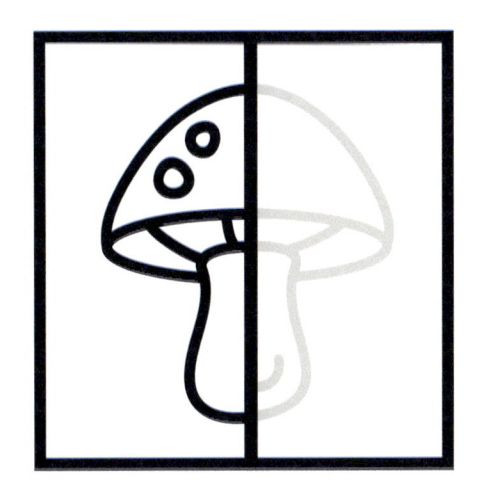

mushroom

For six years sow your fields, and for six years prune your vineyards and gather their crops. Leviticus 25:3

Name _____   Date _____

I AM THANKFUL FOR...

Draw a picture and write down something you are thankful for this year.

I am thankful for

_____

_____

_____

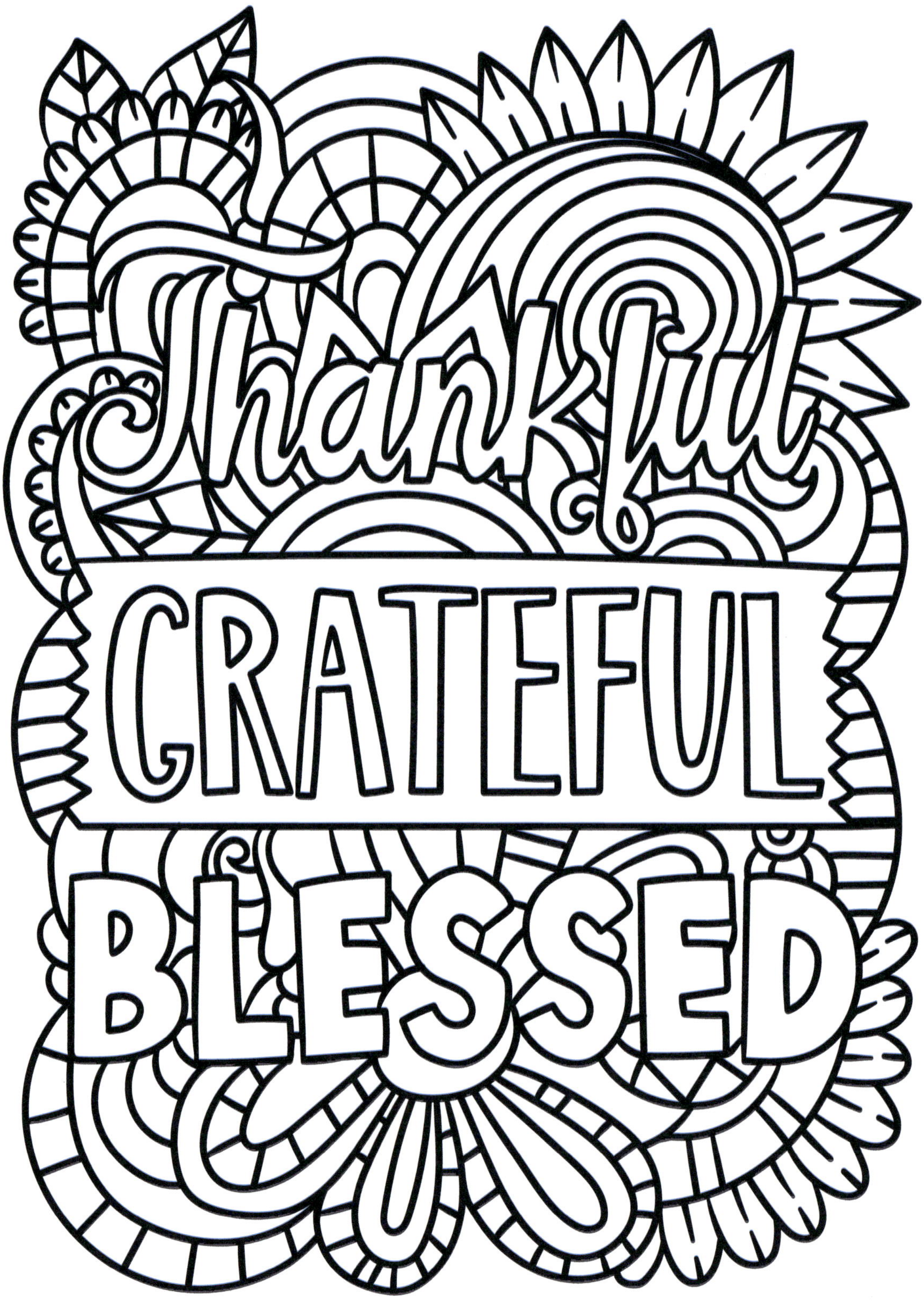
Thankful
GRATEFUL
BLESSED

Name: _____ Date: _____

I Am Thankful For...

Directions: Read the prompt in each box and write your answers.

Something I am thankful for this past year:

Something I am looking forward to next year:

Something I am grateful for about myself:

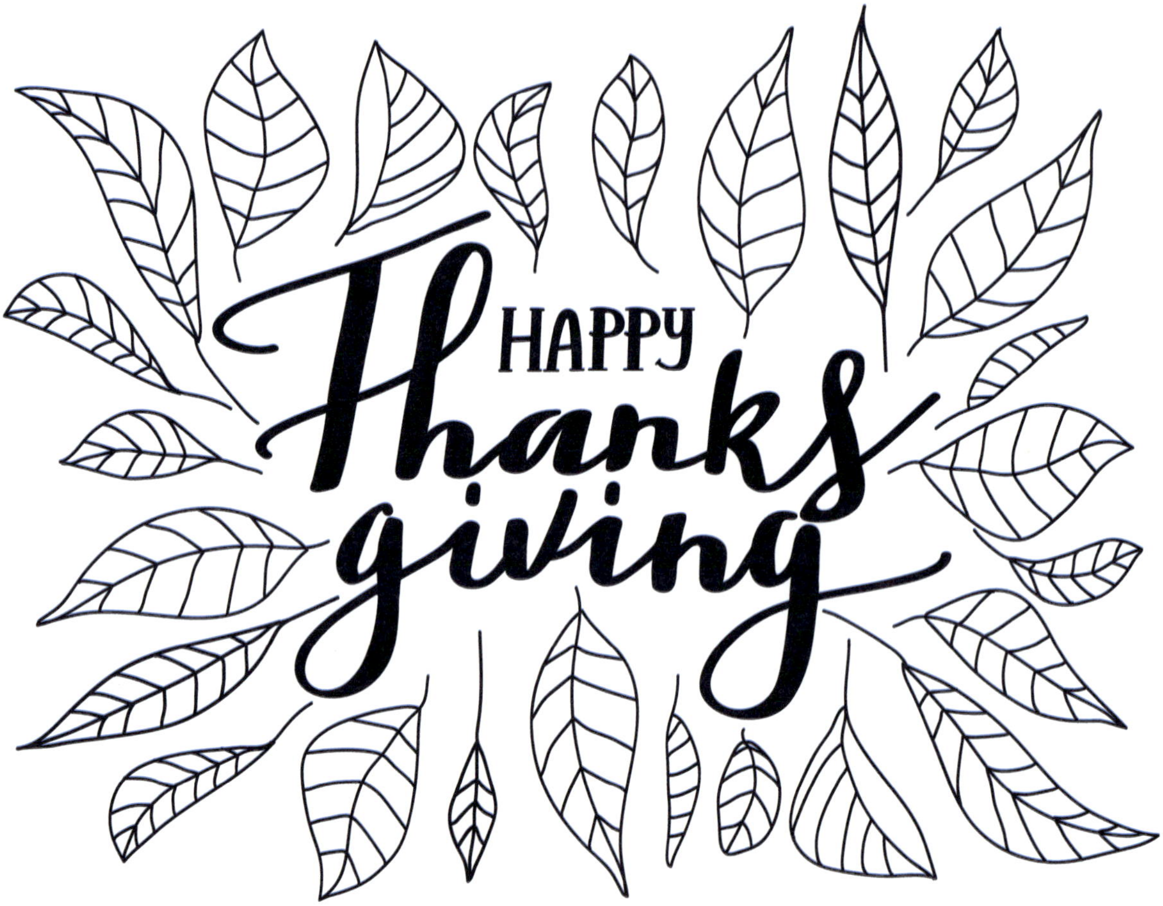
HAPPY
Thanksgiving

A TIME FOR GRATITUDE

Thanksgiving is celebrated on the fourth Thursday of every November, and is one of the most cherished holidays in the United States. But, have you ever wondered what Thanksgiving is really about? It's more than just taking a day off from school or having a feast of delicious food. Thanksgiving is a holiday when people pause and reflect on what they are thankful for. It's a time when family and friends show gratitude to God for all their blessings.

Gratitude is a powerful emotion that not only makes us feel happier but also strengthens our relationships with God & others. When we practice gratitude, we shift our attention away from negative thoughts and emotions, and instead, we acknowledge and cherish the good things.

Expressing gratitude is not only beneficial to ourselves but also to those around us. When we show appreciation to others, it strengthens our relationships and creates a sense of connection. People feel valued and encouraged when they receive heartfelt thanks. This cycle of gratitude can have a ripple effect, spreading positivity and improving the overall well-being of a community.

There are so many ways you can practice gratitude in your life. One simple way is to keep a gratitude journal. Each day, write down three things you are grateful for. It could be something as small as a beautiful sunset or a kind gesture from a friend. By writing them down, you reinforce the positive experiences and train your mind to focus on the good things.

We can also practice gratitude by giving back to our community. Volunteer at a local shelter, donate to a charity, or lend a helping hand to someone in need. These actions remind us of the privileges we have and how we can make a difference in the lives of others.

How will you show your gratitude this fall?

Name _____   Date _____

BIBLE STUDY

Fruits of the Sprirt: Next to each one, write their meaning.

Love _____
_____

Joy _____
_____

Peace _____
_____

Patience _____
_____

Kindness _____
_____

Goodness _____
_____

Gentleness _____
_____

Self Control _____
_____

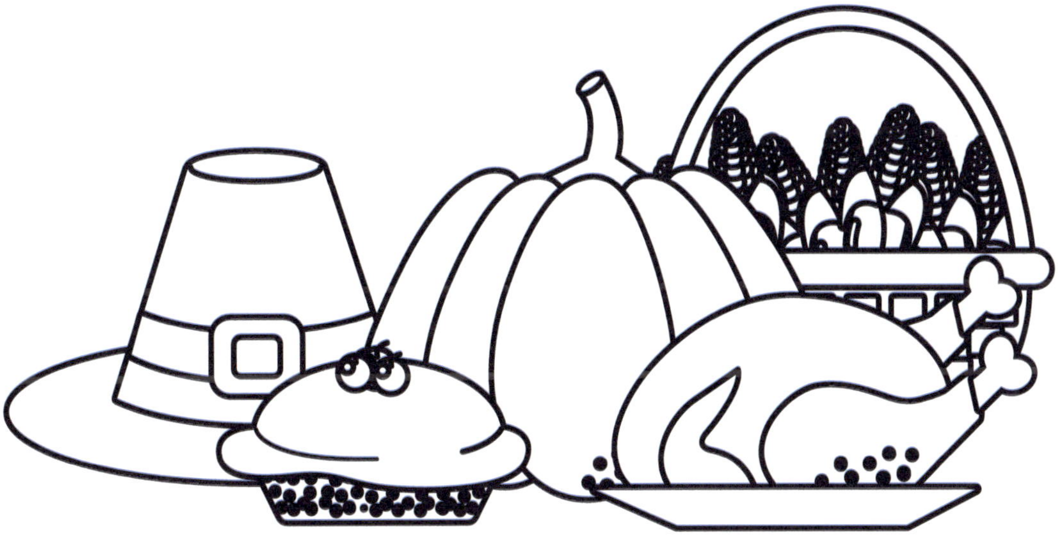

Leviticus 20:25 (NIV)
You must therefore make a distinction between clean and unclean animals and between unclean and clean birds. Do not defile yourselves by any animal or bird or anything that moves along the ground—those that I have set apart as unclean for you.

Turkeys are biblically clean animals!

Count your blessings.

Count each Fall item and then write the correct number in each box.

Count your blessings.

Write something that is a blessing in your life on each pumpkin, then color.

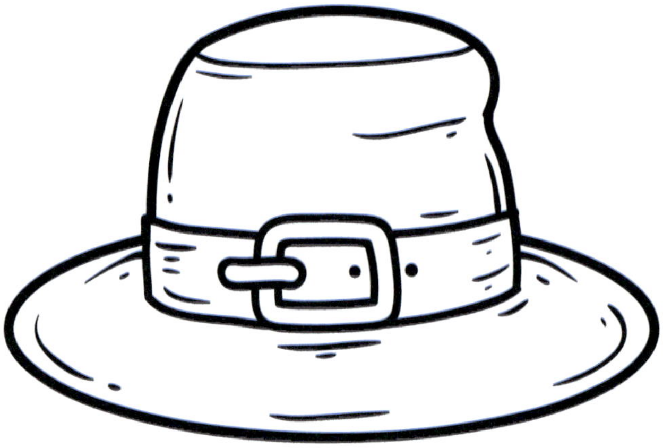

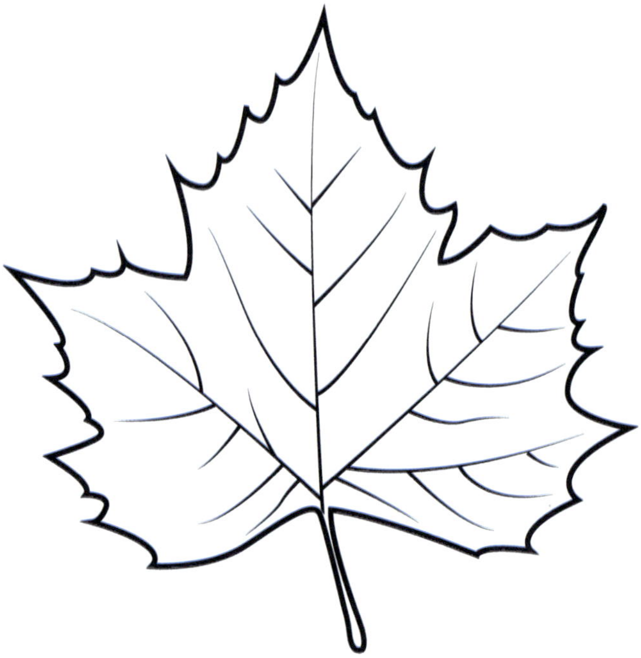

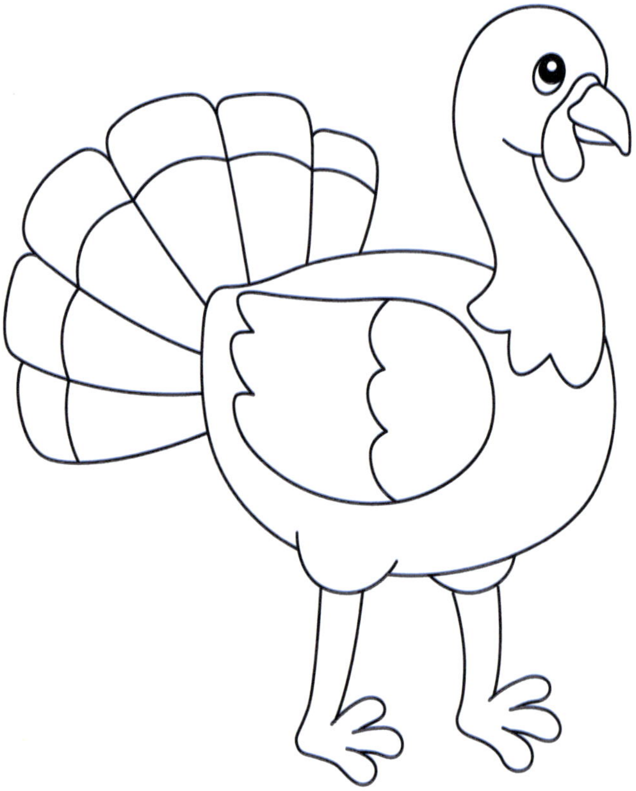

Name _____ Date _____

BIBLE STUDY

Answer the following reading comprehension questions about Leviticus 23.

🎃 What are the holy days listed in Leviticus 23?
_____
_____

🎃 For how long should we celebrate or observe these feasts?
_____
_____

🎃 Who do these feasts belong to?
_____
_____

🎃 Name something we can do today on the Feast of Trumpets?
_____
_____

🎃 What is something we can do today to observe the Feast of Tabernacles?
_____
_____

🎃 Tell me about a time you've gone camping, or a time you've built a fort.
_____
_____

Happy Thanksgiving

Name: _____ Date: _____

MY GRATITUDE JARS

Think about all the people, places, and things you are grateful for. Write or draw what you are grateful for in the jars below.

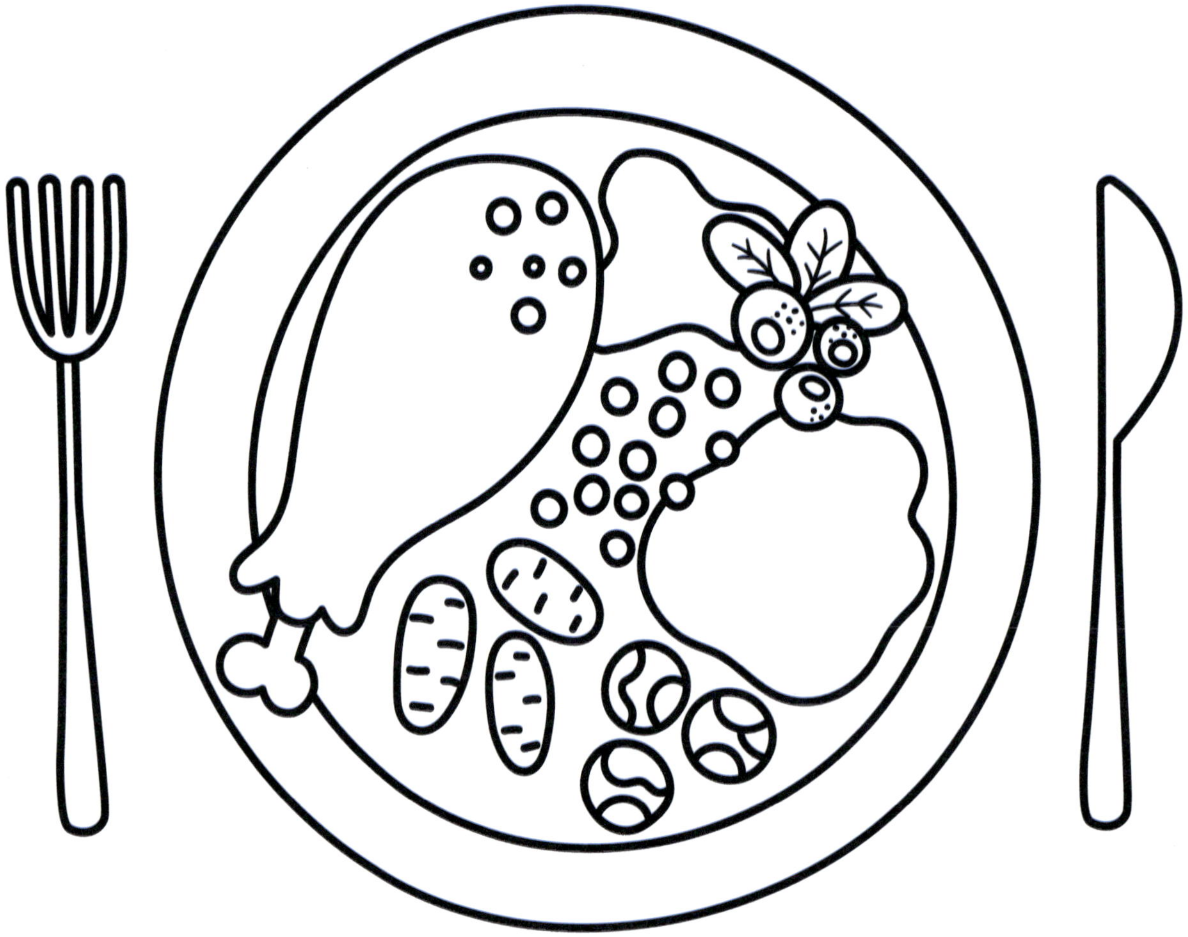

1st Thessalonians 5:16

REJOICE
Always

So don't be afraid; you are worth more than many sparrows. Matthew 10:31

Name: _____ Class: _____

Autumn

Look at the pictures and mark the correct option.

	Leaves / Fruit basket / Maple leaf
	Pumpkin / Hazel nut / Mushroom
	Hazel nut / Fruit basket / Umbrella
	Scarecrow / Mushroom / Boot
	Leaves / Mushroom / Hazel nut
	Sea star / Garden fork / Leaves
	Maple leaf / Umbrella / Fruit basket
	Boot / Scarecrow / Umbrella
	Pumpkin / Boot / Maple leaf
	Fruit basket / Leaves / Boot

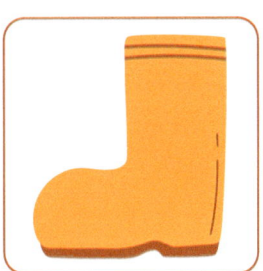

"Come, follow me," Jesus said, "and I will make you fishers of men." Mark 1:17

Name: _____ Score: _____

FALL PATTERN

Draw the object to complete the pattern.

Its leaves were beautiful, its fruit abundant, and on it was food for all. Under it the wild animals found shelter, and the birds lived in its branches; from it every creature was fed.
Daniel 4:12

Name: _____

Counting Leaves

Count the leaves and write it down in the box

FALL VOCABULARY

Fall is a season that falls between summer and winter. In the fall, the temperature cools down, leaves change color, and animals prepare for a long winter.

scarecrow	apple	squirrel	football
cornucopia	acorn	owl	turkey
corn	scarf	leaf	pumpkin

Live in temporary shelters for seven days;
Leviticus 23:42

Name _____   Date _____

FALLING INTO FALL

Read the passage below to learn about fall in the United States, then answer the questions on the next page.

Autumn, also known as fall, is one of the four seasons. It comes after summer and before winter. During this season, the days become shorter, and the nights get longer. Leaves change from green to shades of red, orange, yellow, and brown before they fall off the trees.

Fall is known for its festivals and traditions. One of the most popular holidays in fall is Thanksgiving, which happens in November. During Thanksgiving, there is usually a large feast with family and friends, typically served with turkey where prayers of gratitude are made to God. In some places, people also hold harvest festivals to celebrate the food and crops they've grown. Additionally, there's a growing number of people celebrating the biblical holidays, where they blow trumpets, feast then fast, then camp!

Fall is a time for harvesting. This means farmers collect the crops they've grown over the summer. Some of the popular fall crops are apples, pumpkins, corn, and squash. These foods are used in delicious dishes like apple pies, pumpkin muffins, and roasted corn.

Not only is the food great, but the weather is too. Fall weather is often cool and crisp, but not too cold. It's perfect for wearing cozy sweaters and scarves. The cool air also makes it easier to be active outside, like playing football or going on nature walks.

Fall is also a busy time for animals. Many animals prepare for winter by collecting food and making their homes warmer. Squirrels, for instance, gather nuts and store them to eat during the cold months. Some birds fly south to warmer places.

In conclusion, fall is a season full of changes and preparations. Whether you're getting ready for the upcoming holidays or an animal preparing for winter, there's always something happening in autumn!

Name _____   Date _____

FALLING INTO FALL

Use context clues to determine the meaning of the following words.

1. traditions _____
   _____

2. harvesting _____
   _____

3. Thanksgiving _____
   _____

4. gratitude _____
   _____

5. crisp _____
   _____

6. cozy _____
   _____

7. preparations _____
   _____

8. festivals _____
   _____

Name _____   Date _____

FALLING INTO FALL

Answer the following reading comprehension questions about the passage.

🍁 What happens to the length of days and nights during the fall season?
_____
_____

🍁 What traditions occur in the fall?
_____
_____

🍁 Why do people hold harvest festivals?
_____
_____

🍁 Why do people try to stay cozy in the fall?
_____
_____

🍁 Why do animals, like squirrels, gather and store food during autumn?
_____
_____

🍁 Based on the passage, how can you tell that fall is a season of preparation?
_____
_____

Pumpkins are orange.

Thanks giving

FALL LEAVES

Solve the equations below and then color the leaves using the key provided at the bottom of this page.

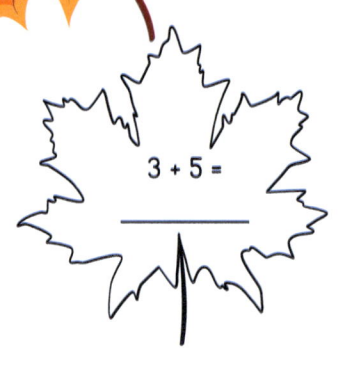

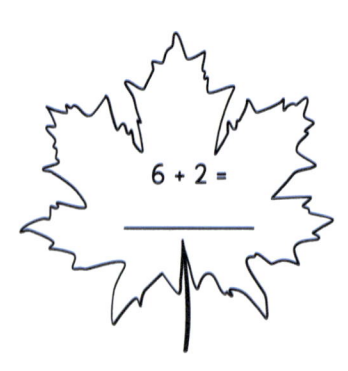

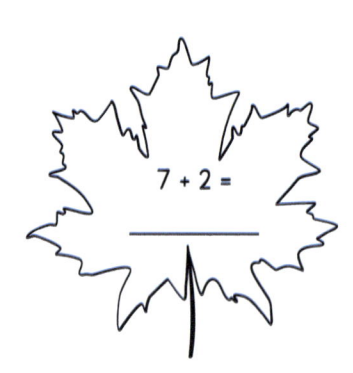

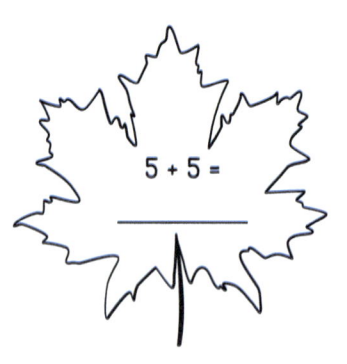

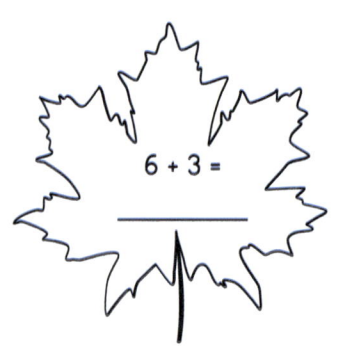

3 + 5 = ____

2 + 4 = ____

6 + 2 = ____

3 + 7 = ____

7 + 2 = ____

5 + 5 = ____

7 + 1 = ____

1 + 5 = ____

6 + 3 = ____

6 Yellow   9 Red
8 Orange   10 Brown

Name:

COUNT YOUR BLESSINGS

Count each picture and write the number of each below.

🎃 = ◯   🎃 = ◯

🌰 = ◯   🍂 = ◯

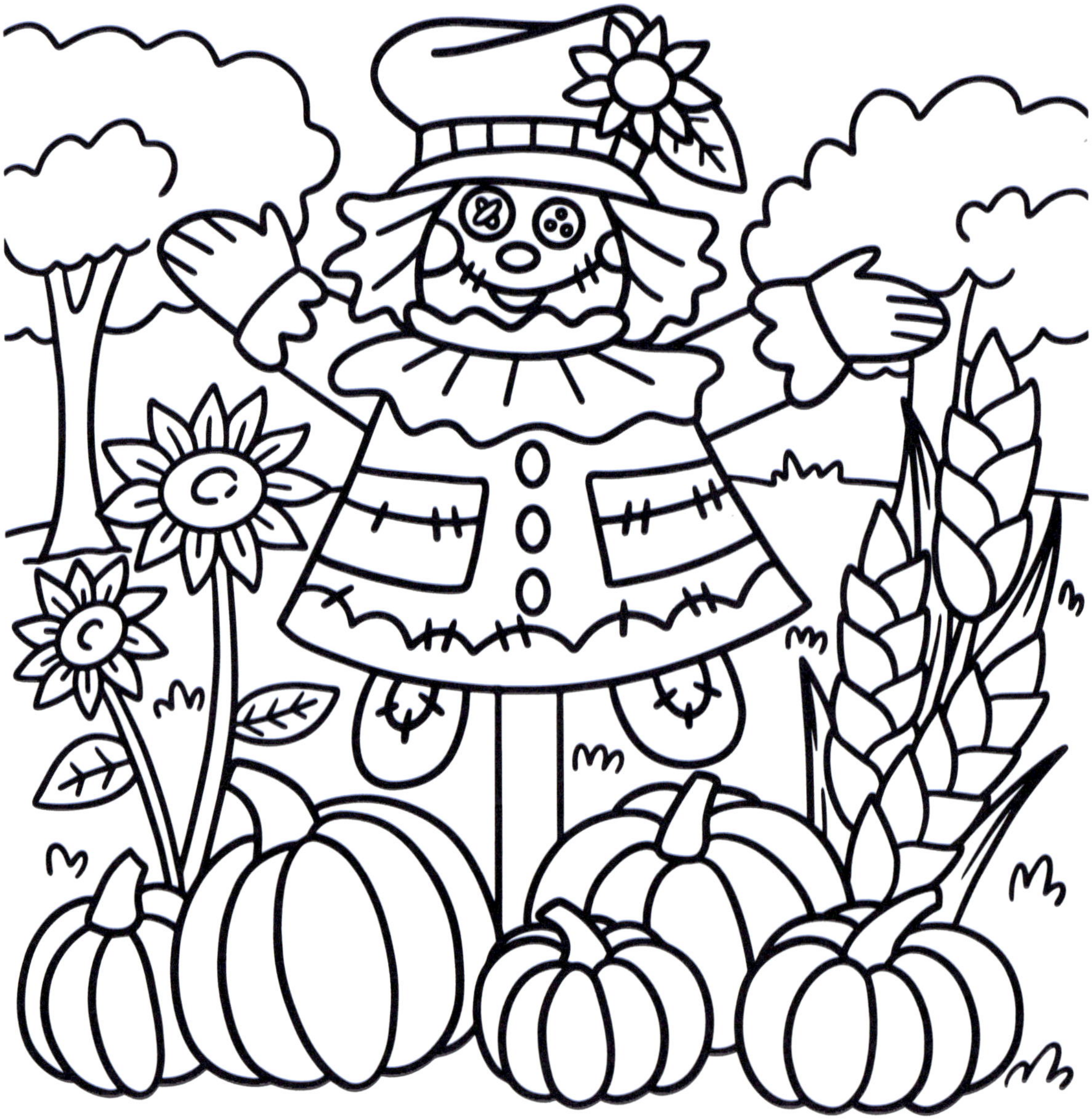

Name: Date:

Autumn Addition

2 + 3 =

3 + 3 =

5 + 3 =

3 + 2 =

AUTUMN PUMPKIN

Color the pumpkin using shades of orange, brown and green.

Word Search
THANKSGIVING FOOD

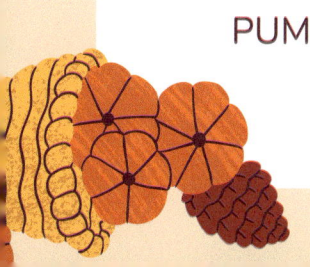

Find the hidden names of the Thanksgiving Food.

```
P N M T O I C A N U C C
U S T U F F I N G H O R
M Q W R C A J T A A R A
P U D K A N C A U N N N
K A A E G R A V Y U B B
I S P Y A S S I T S R E
N H P E D V S A R A E R
P M L T I E A N A P A R
I P E B C B R E A D D Y
E I P A O U O W I T N E
G R I E R E L I A K T S
G R E E N B E A N S E G
```

APPLE PIE	CORN	BREAD	CASSEROLE
STUFFING	GRAVY	TURKEY	CRANBERRY
PUMPKIN PIE	CORNBREAD	SQUASH	GREEN BEANS

Answer Key
THANKSGIVING FOOD

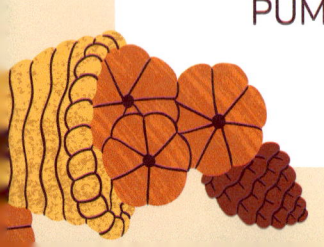

Find the hidden names of the Thanksgiving Food.

```
P N M T O I C A N U C C
U S T U F F I N G H O R
M Q W R C A J T A A R A
P U D K A N C A U N N N
K A A E G R A V Y U B B
I S P Y A S S I T S R E
N H P E D V S A R A E R
P M L T I E A N A P A R
I P E B C B R E A D D Y
E I P A O U O W I T N E
  G R I E R E L I A K T S
  G R E E N B E A N S E G
```

APPLE PIE	CORN	BREAD	CASSEROLE
STUFFING	GRAVY	TURKEY	CRANBERRY
PUMPKIN PIE	CORNBREAD	SQUASH	GREEN BEANS

Name: _____   Date: _____

Three Words Game

Think of three words for each category. You can write them or say them.

Months of autumn	Colors of autumn leaves	Weather in autumn
_____	_____	_____
_____	_____	_____
_____	_____	_____

Clothes people usually wear in autumn	Food people usually eat in autumn	Activities people usually do in autumn
_____	_____	_____
_____	_____	_____
_____	_____	_____

Fruits and vegetables in season for autumn	Festivals that take place in autumn	Things you love about autumn
_____	_____	_____
_____	_____	_____
_____	_____	_____

Birthdays celebrated in autumn	Autumn characteristics	Things you don't like about autumn
_____	_____	_____
_____	_____	_____
_____	_____	_____

AUTUMN WORD SCRAMBLE

Unscramble the following autumn words

TEER　　　　　_____

LAFE　　　　　_____

WNID　　　　　_____

ARNOC　　　　_____

LAEVSE　　　 _____

BESKAT　　　 _____

ALPEPS　　　 _____

PIUMKPN　　　_____

MSHUOORM　　_____

UBREMALL　　_____

HRAVETS　　　_____

PLEI FO LAEVES　_____

Name: _____   Date: _____

Autumn Patterns

Can you complete each autumn pattern? Cut and glue

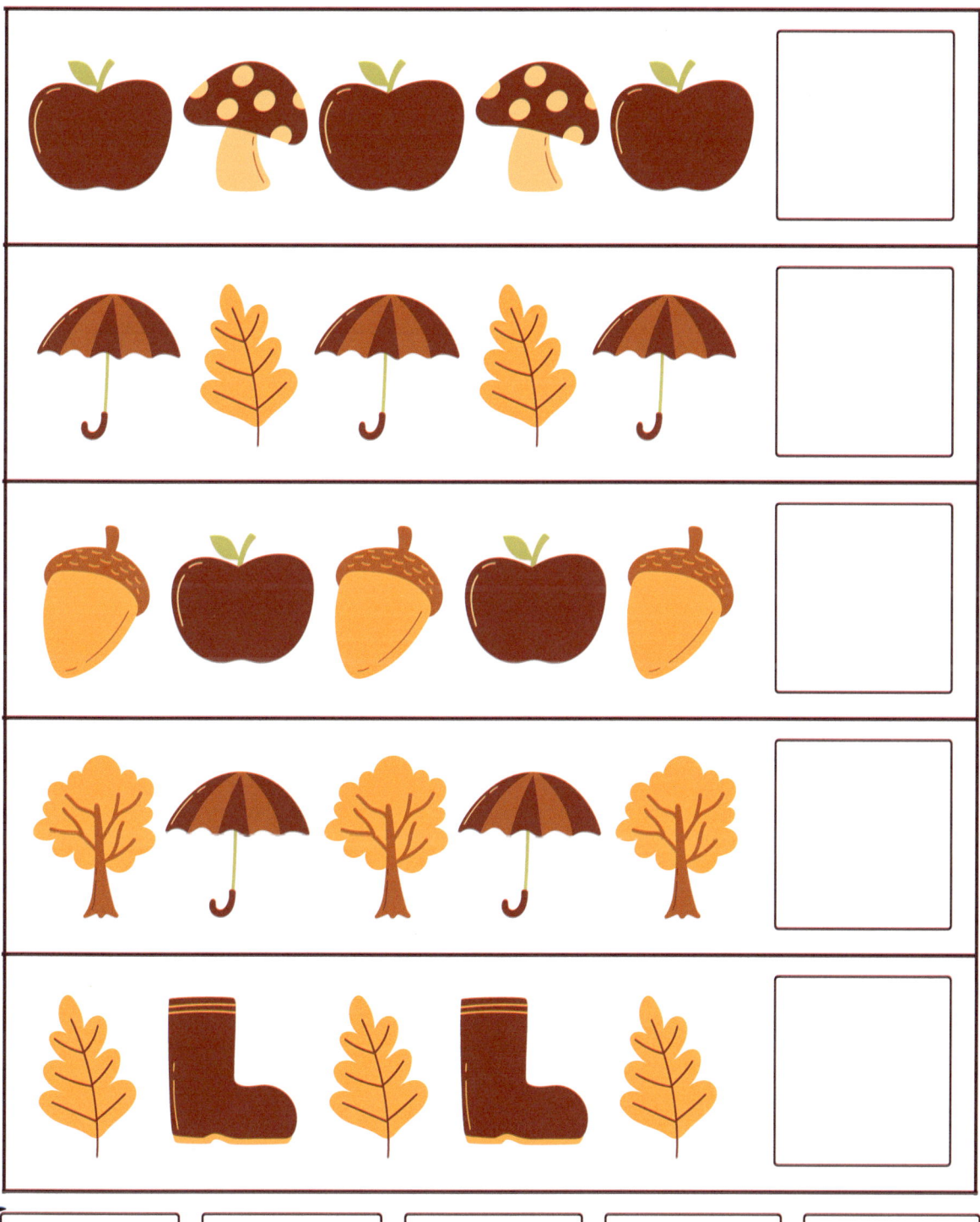

Name: _____ Date: _____

AUTUMN
WORD SCRAMBLE

Unscramble the following autumn words

TEER	TREE
LAFE	LEAF
WNID	WIND
ARNOC	ACORN
LAEVSE	LEAVES
BESKAT	BASKET
ALPEPS	APPLES
PIUMKPN	PUMPKIN
MSHUOORM	MUSHROOM
UBREMALL	UMBRELLA
HRAVETS	HARVEST
PLEI FO LAEVES	PILE OF LEAVES

Name: _____   Date: _____

AUTUMN LEAVES

Draw and color yellow, orange, brown, and red leaves on the tree.

MY GRATITUDE TREE
BY _____

Write all the people, places, and things you are grateful for in the leaves of this tree.

GRATITUDE
WORD SEARCH

Find and circle all the words to be grateful for.

WARMTH	JOY	FREEDOM	PARTIES
PETS	LOVE	SCHOOL	FOOD
SEASONS	GAMES	FRIENDS	FAMILY

```
Q B F F R I E N D S
S W F Q S E A V S W
C A R P E D J P C A
E R E B A G N V H M
P M E F S R Z D O I
E T D O O O T U O L
T H O O N T N I L Y
S J M D S Y J L E X
G A M E S L O V E S
N V T S B P Y T Z W
```

THANKSGIVING
word search

Can you find all the words related to Thanksgiving?

f	r	f	e	d	k	x	t	r	h	v	a	r	k	i
m	o	l	n	a	e	b	u	x	p	n	a	i	s	b
g	y	o	x	b	h	u	r	l	u	h	o	u	j	d
u	f	b	t	k	p	q	k	v	i	s	k	u	z	x
d	e	u	h	b	p	i	e	x	s	a	i	m	b	n
b	y	l	i	m	a	f	y	t	w	u	q	m	i	p
d	j	r	w	o	s	l	u	m	e	q	u	k	o	s
s	i	c	r	p	o	f	l	l	e	s	p	t	m	l
d	l	n	m	e	f	a	h	o	t	m	a	n	u	l
e	a	f	n	i	b	k	w	d	u	t	o	q	x	o
z	h	l	n	e	t	n	z	p	o	u	f	j	h	r
i	o	g	a	j	r	a	a	e	d	a	r	a	p	i
j	v	r	m	s	p	e	s	r	o	u	s	w	n	s
y	x	i	s	o	r	a	p	h	c	j	x	c	k	y
f	m	o	w	b	z	x	s	d	h	k	b	l	u	p

cranberry   football   pumpkin   squash

dinner   parade   pumpkin   stuffing

family   pie   rolls   turkey

Name: Grade: Date:

I am Thankful

Complete the leaves with things you are thankful for

ANSWER SHEET

f	r	f	e	d	k	x	t	r	h	v	a	r	k	i
m	o	l	n	a	e	b	u	x	p	n	a	i	s	b
g	y	o	x	b	h	u	r	l	u	h	o	u	j	d
u	f	b	t	k	p	q	k	v	i	s	k	u	z	x
d	e	u	h	b	p	i	e	x	s	a	i	m	b	n
b	y	l	i	m	a	f	y	t	w	u	q	m	i	p
d	j	r	w	o	s	l	u	m	e	q	u	k	o	s
s	i	c	r	p	o	f	l	l	e	s	p	t	m	l
d	l	n	m	e	f	a	h	o	t	m	a	n	u	l
e	a	f	n	i	b	k	w	d	u	t	o	q	x	o
z	h	l	n	e	t	n	z	p	o	u	f	j	h	r
i	o	g	a	j	r	a	a	e	d	a	r	a	p	i
j	v	r	m	s	p	e	s	r	o	u	s	w	n	s
y	x	i	s	o	r	a	p	h	c	j	x	c	k	y
f	m	o	w	b	z	x	s	d	h	k	b	l	u	p

cranberry	football	pumpkin	squash
dinner	parade	potatoes	stuffing
family	pie	rolls	turkey

Name: _____ Date: _____

AUTUMN WORD SEARCH

Find the words below in the word search.

S	A	S	P	D	B	F	G	C	E	A	H
C	S	Q	U	I	R	R	E	L	J	C	I
A	K	U	M	L	A	M	N	E	P	O	S
R	Y	A	P	W	K	V	H	A	U	R	T
E	Z	S	K	A	E	B	A	F	C	N	J
C	L	H	I	J	H	G	R	A	I	N	A
R	K	M	N	K	I	G	V	E	F	D	C
O	P	N	H	E	D	G	E	H	O	G	K
W	Q	S	R	T	U	X	S	W	Q	Y	E
C	H	E	S	T	N	U	T	A	D	Z	T

SQUIRREL   CHESTNUT   SCARECROW
ACORN   HARVEST   RAKE
PUMPKIN   RAIN   SQUASH
LEAF   HEDGEHOG   JACKET

GRATITUDE JOURNAL

by:

_____

A TIME FOR GRATITUDE

Write in this gratitude journal daily in the month of November to express your gratitude for others and the world around you. There is one sentence prompt for every day of the month.

Write about someone who made you smile today and why they're amazing.
_____
_____
_____

What's something beautiful you saw outside today that made you feel thankful?
_____
_____
_____

What's one thing you're looking forward to this month?
_____
_____
_____

Write about an accomplishment that made you feel proud.
_____
_____
_____

A TIME FOR GRATITUDE

Write in this gratitude journal daily in the month of November to express your gratitude for others and the world around you. There is one sentence prompt for every day of the month.

Write about a hobby or activity that you enjoy and why it's special to you.
_____
_____
_____

Describe a person who makes your day better just by being themselves.
_____
_____
_____

What's a lesson you learned from a mistake or a tough situation this week?
_____
_____
_____

What's the best advice you've ever received and how have you used it in your life?
_____
_____
_____

A TIME FOR GRATITUDE

Write in this gratitude journal daily in the month of November to express your gratitude for others and the world around you. There is one sentence prompt for every day of the month.

What is something you use every day that you're thankful for? Why is it important?

_____
_____
_____

Write about a hobby or activity that you enjoy and why it's special to you.

_____
_____
_____

Write about what freedom means to you and why you appreciate it.

_____
_____
_____

Share a memory that makes you happy whenever you think about it.

_____
_____
_____

A TIME FOR GRATITUDE

Write in this gratitude journal daily in the month of November to express your gratitude for others and the world around you. There is one sentence prompt for every day of the month.

What's a nice thing someone said to you or you said to someone else?

_____

_____

_____

Did anything surprise you today in a good way? Why did it feel special?

_____

_____

_____

Before Thanksgiving, write about three things you're most grateful for this year.

_____

_____

_____

What's a tradition you enjoy during Thanksgiving time?

_____

_____

_____

A TIME FOR GRATITUDE

Look back on the month and write about your favorite moments of gratitude. What were you the most grateful for? Who helped you feel grateful? How did you show others you were grateful, and what happened? What lessons did you learn?

_____
_____
_____
_____
_____
_____
_____
_____
_____
_____
_____
_____
_____
_____
_____

I AM GRATEFUL FOR

Showing gratitude helps you appreciate all the things in your life. When you're grateful, you take a moment to say "thank you" for the people, things, and experiences that make you happy. Write down one thing that makes you happy for each letter of the alphabet.

a _____
b _____
c _____
d _____
e _____
f _____
g _____
h _____
i _____
j _____
k _____
l _____
m _____

n _____
o _____
p _____
q _____
r _____
s _____
t _____
u _____
v _____
w _____
x _____
y _____
z _____

Name: Date:

I Am Thankful For...

Directions: Read the prompt in each box and write your answers.

Something I am thankful for at home:

Something I am thankful for at school:

Someone I am thankful for:

Name: Date:

I AM THANKFUL FOR...

Write something or name someone you are thankful for in each maple leaf.

Let's count in Autumn!

Count and write your answers in the boxes below

Thanksgiving Maths

Count the Thanksgiving item and write the number in the box.

Thanksgiving Maths

Count the Thanksgiving item and write the number in the box.

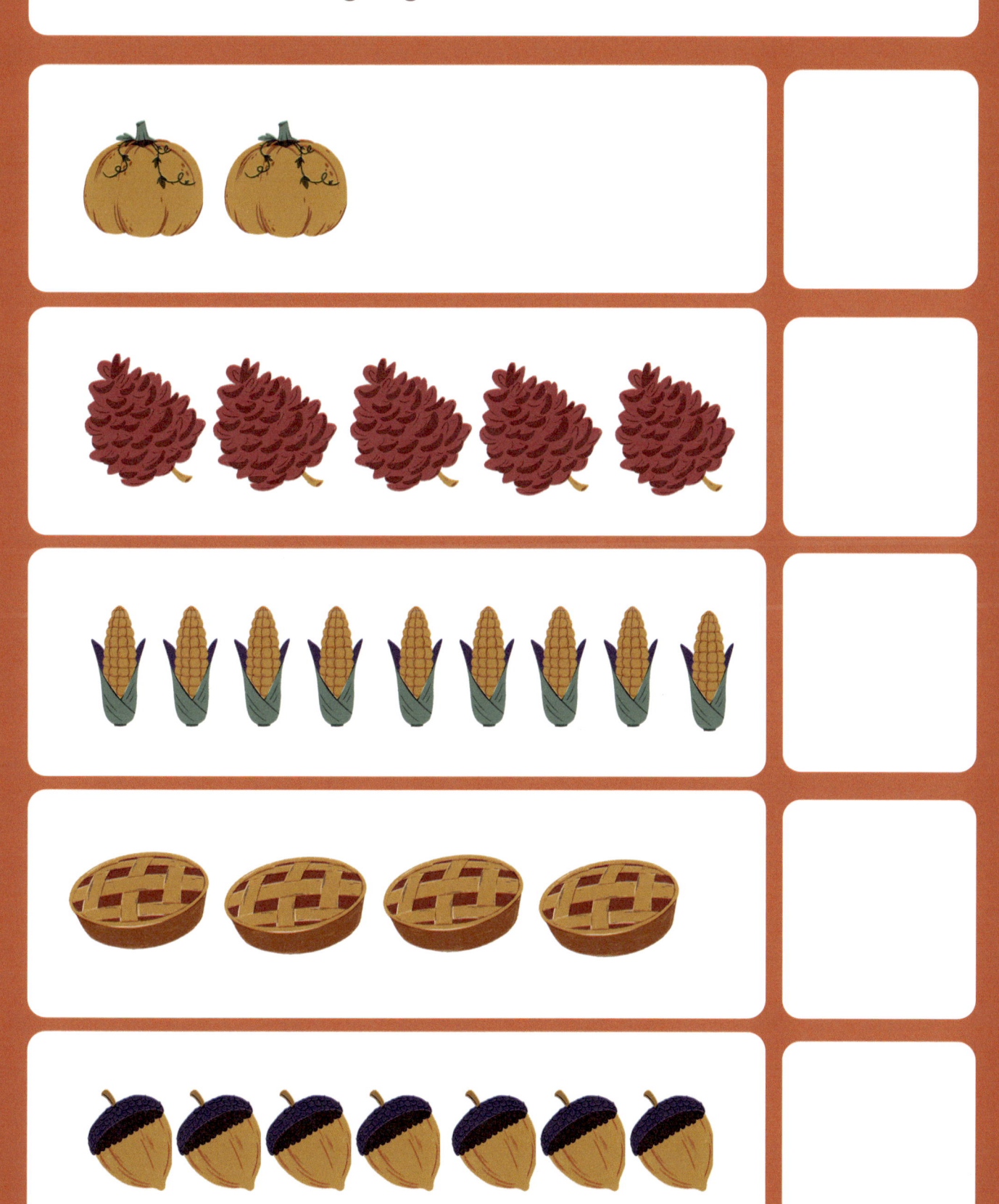

ANSWER KEY

🥧🥧🥧🥧	4
🦃	1
🍁🍁🍁🍁🍁	5
🌰🌰🌰🌰🌰🌰🌰	7
🎩🎩🎩	3

Thanksgiving Maths

Count the Thanksgiving item and write the number in the box.

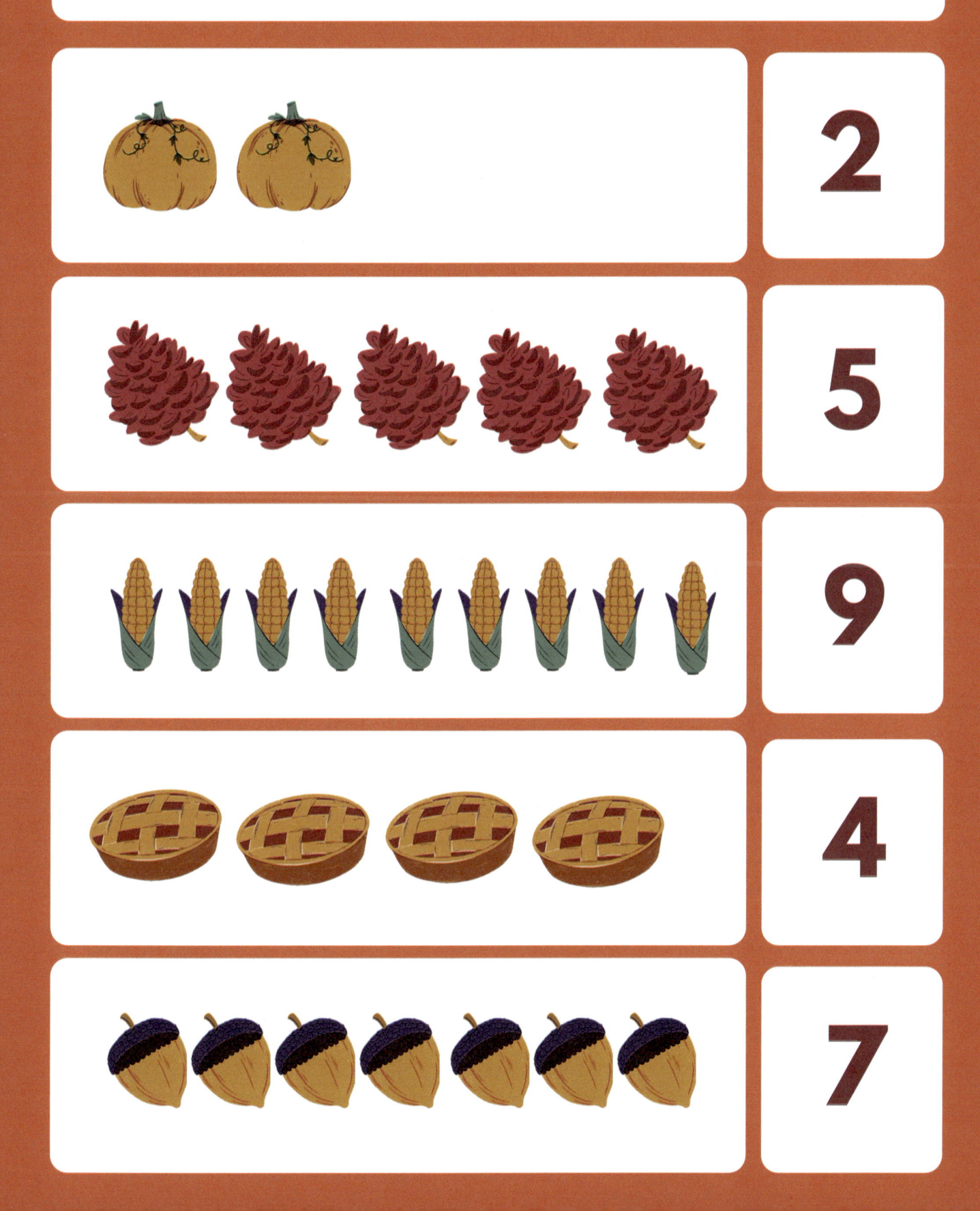

🎃🎃	2
🌰🌰🌰🌰🌰	5
🌽🌽🌽🌽🌽🌽🌽🌽🌽	9
🥧🥧🥧🥧	4
🌰🌰🌰🌰🌰🌰🌰	7

Name: _____   Date: _____

Autumn is here!

Look at the pictures and write the words in the correct place

Pile of leaves	Umbrella	Leaf	Leaves
Mushrooms	Pumpkin	Trees	Basket
Hot drinks	Acorn	Apple	Boots

I AM THANKFUL FOR YOU!

Name _____ Date _____

AUTUMN VOCABULARY

Identify the pictures below. Use the word bank below to name each picture.

Word Bank:

| acorn | apple | mushroom | leaf |

Name _____ Date _____

AUTUMN VOCABULARY

Identify the pictures below. Use the word bank below to name each picture.

Word Bank:

| pie | deer | pumpkin | squirrel |

Name _____   Date _____

SENTENCE WRITING

Look at the picture below. Write a sentence that tells about the picture.

Name _____   Date _____

SENTENCE WRITING

Look at the picture below. Write a sentence that tells about the picture.

Name _____   Date _____

SENTENCE WRITING

Look at the picture below. Write a sentence that tells about the picture.

Name _____ Date _____

SENTENCE WRITING

Look at the picture below. Write a sentence that tells about the picture.

Name _____ Date _____

SENTENCE WRITING

Look at the picture below. Write a sentence that tells about the picture.

Name _____   Date _____

SENTENCE WRITING

Look at the picture below. Write a sentence that tells about the picture.

Name _____ Date _____

SENTENCE WRITING

Look at the picture below. Write a sentence that tells about the picture.

_____
_____
_____
_____

Name _____   Date _____

SENTENCE WRITING

Look at the picture below. Write a sentence that tells about the picture.

....

....

....

....

....

Name _____ Date _____

SENTENCE WRITING

Look at the picture below. Write a sentence that tells about the picture.

_____
_____
_____
_____
_____

Name _____   Date _____

SENTENCE WRITING

Look at the picture below. Write a sentence that tells about the picture.

_____
....
_____
....
_____
....
_____

Name _____ Date _____

FALL FUN

What is your favorite fall activity?

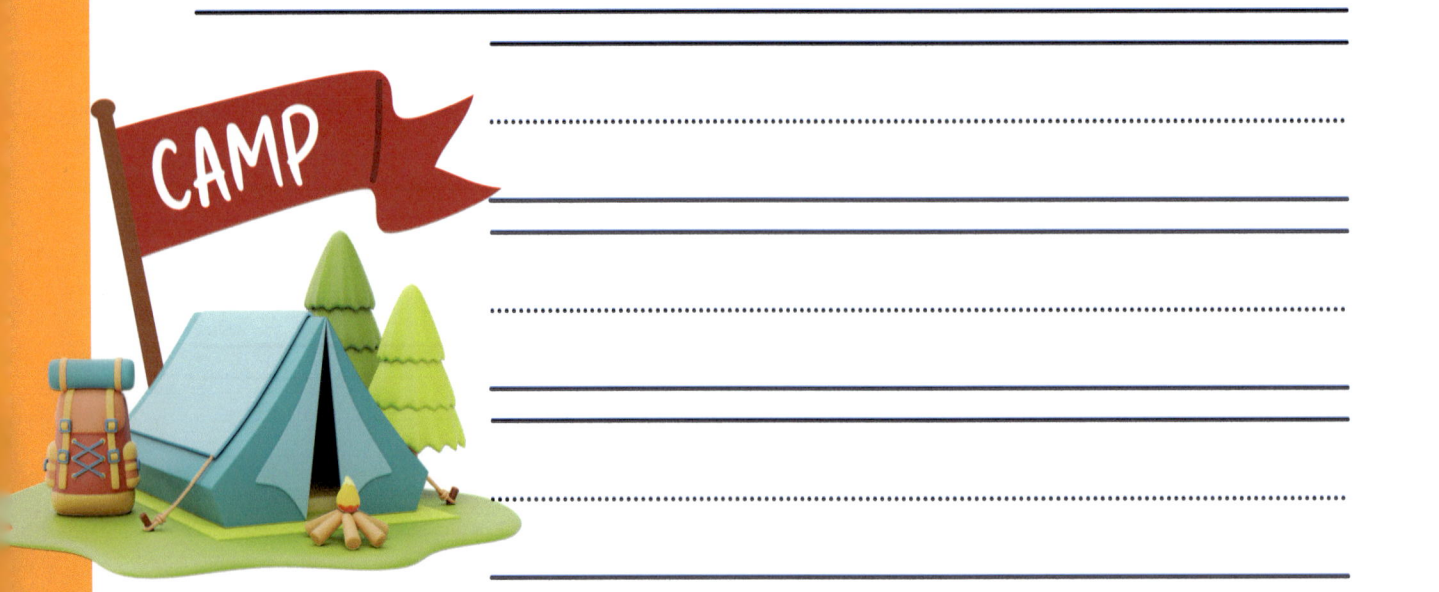

_____
....
_____
_____
....
_____
_____
....
_____
_____
....
_____
_____
....
_____
             _____
             ....
             _____
             _____
             ....
             _____

CAMP

Name _____   Date _____

FALLS'S BEST THING

What is the best thing about fall?

Name _____ Date _____

MY FALL FAVORITES

What fall activity do you love to do?

Name _____ Date _____

MY FALL RECIPE

Do you help cook during a feast? What is your recipe?

Name _____   Date _____

AUTUMN COUNTING

Find and count the following items.

Name _____ Date _____

AUTUMN COUNTING

Count the apples and circle the correct number.

Name _____ Date _____

AUTUMN GRAPH

Find and graph the items listed. Then answer the questions below.

How many of each?

Which item did you find the most of? _____

Which item did you find the least of? _____

Name: _____ Date: _____

Positive Affirmation Handwriting Practice

I can be anything I want to be when I grow up.

Practice Time!

Name: Date:

Positive Affirmation Handwriting Practice

Rejoice in the Lord always. Again, I say, rejoice!

Practice Time!

Name: Date:
_____

Positive Affirmation
Handwriting Practice

Look to the Lord and his strength; seek His face always.

Practice Time!

Name: _____   Date: _____

Positive Affirmation
Handwriting Practice

Let everything that has breath praise the Lord.

Practice Time!

Name: Date:

Positive Affirmation Handwriting Practice

When I am afraid,
I put my trust in the
Lord.

Practice Time!

Name: Date:

Positive Affirmation Handwriting Practice

Trust in the Lord
and do good.

Practice Time!

Name: Date:

Positive Affirmation Handwriting Practice

Whatever you do, do it all for the glory of God.

Practice Time!

Name: Date:

Positive Affirmation Handwriting Practice

Do unto others as you would have them do unto you.

Practice Time!

Name: Date:

Positive Affirmation Handwriting Practice

Trust in the Lord
with all you heart.

Practice Time!

CANDY CORN SKIP COUNTING

Practice your skip counting by fives by tracing the numbers below. When you are finished color the candy corn on the back of this page.

5 10 15 20 25

30 35 40 45 50

55 60 65 70 75

80 85 90 95 100

Gratitude Letter

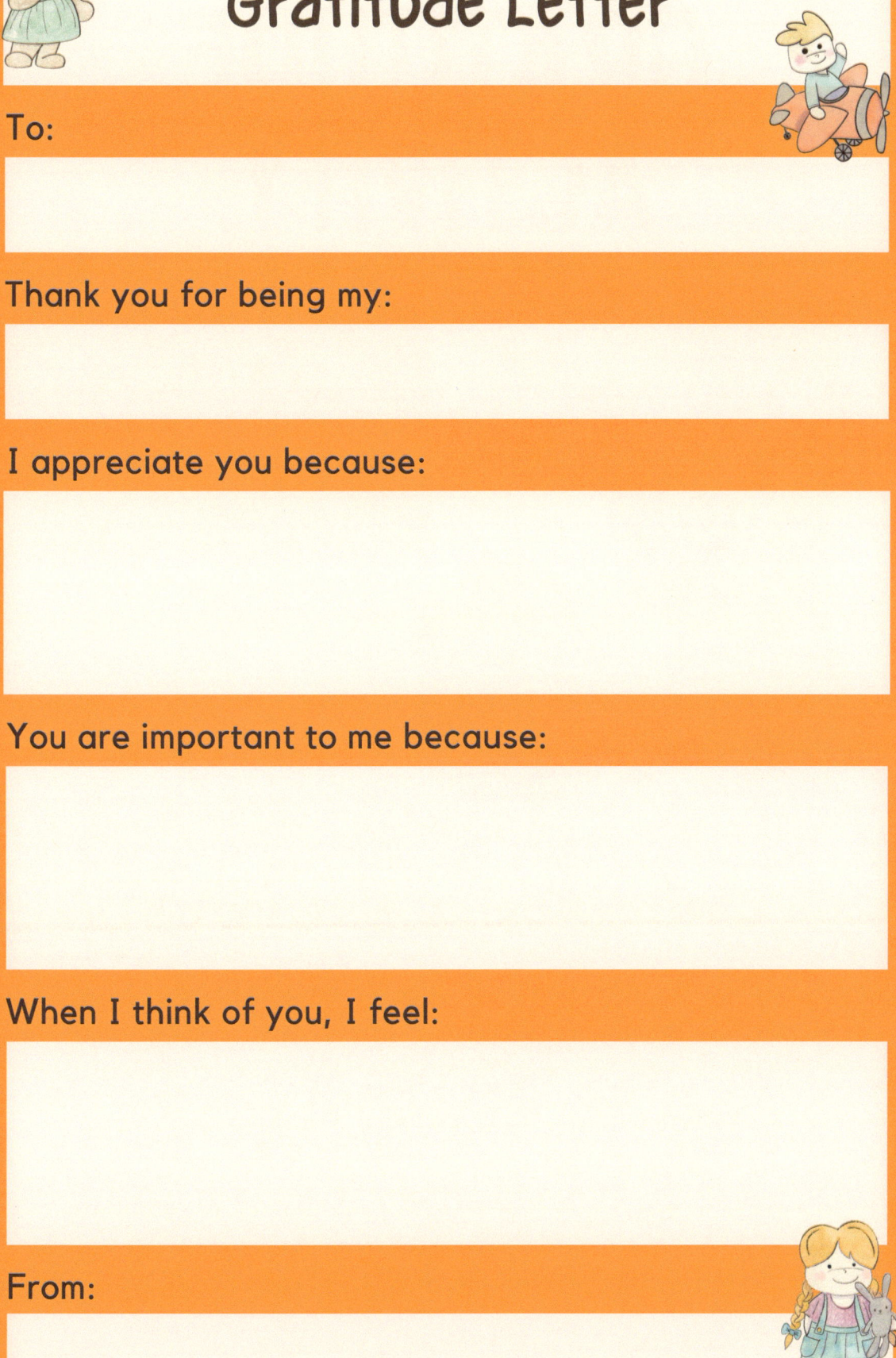

To:

Thank you for being my:

I appreciate you because:

You are important to me because:

When I think of you, I feel:

From:

GRATITUDE ACTIVITY

Name a person you are grateful for. Think about why you are thankful for this person and how this person made you feel.

How did you feel during this task? How can you show gratitude and respect through actions?

GRATITUDE ACTIVITY

Name a situation you are grateful for. Think about why you are thankful for this situation and how remembering it makes you feel.

How did you feel during this task? How can you show gratitude and respect through actions?

GRATITUDE ACTIVITY

Name a thing you are grateful for. Think about why you are thankful for this object and how having it makes you feel.

How did you feel during this task? How can you show gratitude and respect through actions?

GRATEFUL TO BE ME

Draw yourself.

What is something you are grateful for about yourself? Why?

Three things you love about yourself:

GRATEFUL FOR NATURE

Draw your favorite place in nature.

What is your favorite activity to do outdoors?

Which season are you most grateful for?

What animal are you most grateful for?

GRATEFUL FOR MY FAMILY

How does your family make your life better?

Draw a family member you are grateful for.

What is something unique about your family that you are thankful for?

GRATEFUL FOR MY HOME

What is your favorite place at home?

Draw your favorite place at home.

What are your favorite things at home?

GRATEFUL FOR MY FRIENDS

What are the names of your friends?

Draw a friend you are grateful for.

What are you grateful for about your friends?

PEOPLE I AM GRATEFUL FOR

List six people you are grateful for. They can be family, friends, or strangers.

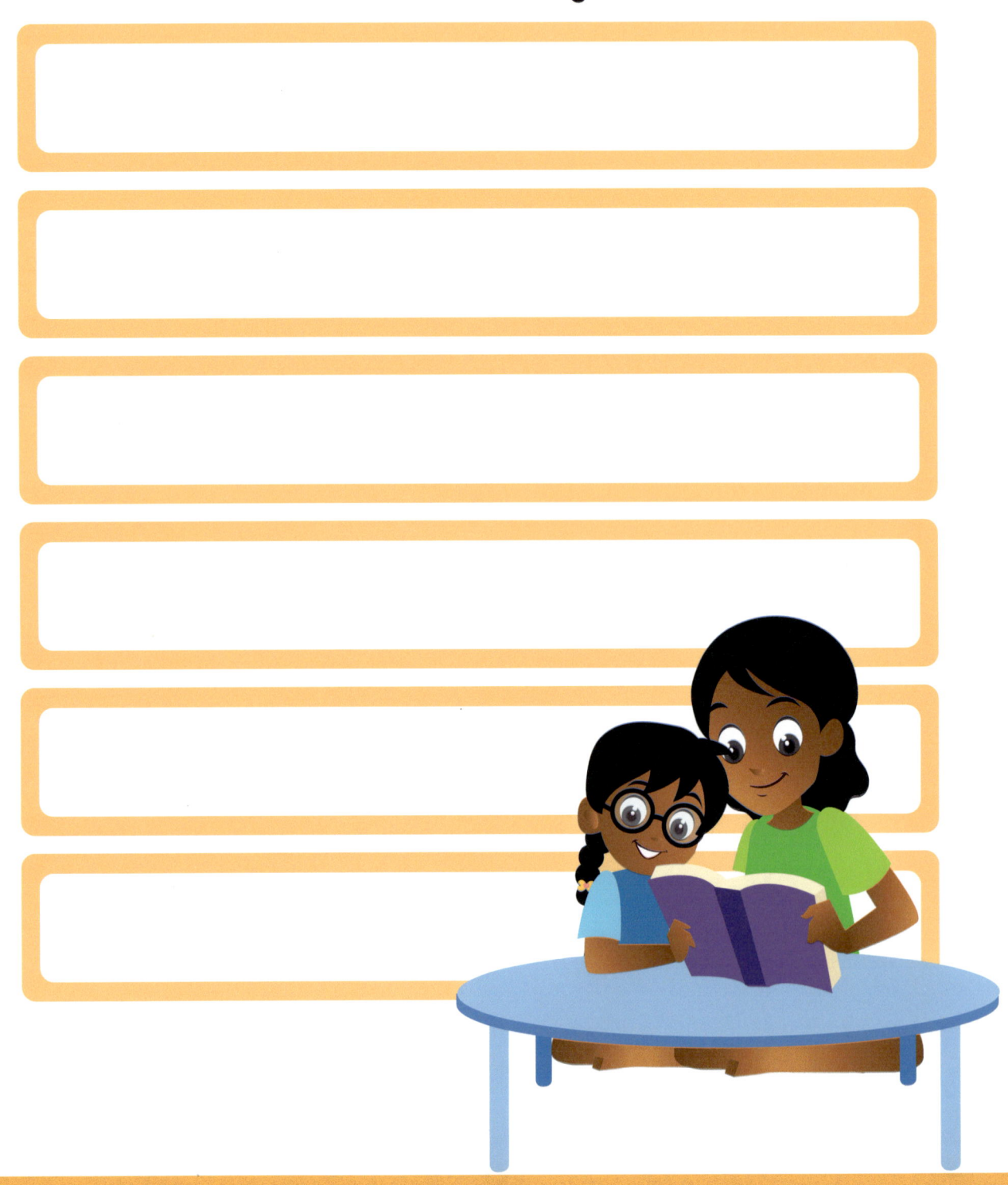

FEELING GRATEFUL

Who or what are you thankful for?

Why are you thankful for this?

How can you give back?

THE THINGS I LOVE

What I love about myself

What I love about my family

What I love about my school

I love this color

I love this smell

I love this weather

THANK YOU!

Think of someone in your life that you'd like to thank. Write a message and tell them what they did and how they made you feel.

DAILY GRATITUDE

Date: _____

Three moments you're grateful for

One person you're grateful to have in your life:

One amazing thing that happened today:

One thing you accomplished today:

One thing you're looking forward to:

DAILY GRATITUDE

Date: _____

Experiences you're thankful for

What is your positive word of the day?

Color in your current mood:

happy   confused   sad

scared   tired   upset

WEEKLY GRATITUDE

Write about something you are thankful for each day.

Monday

Tuesday

Wednesday

Thursday

Friday

Saturday

Sunday

WEEKLY GRATITUDE

Write how you can demonstrate one fruit of the Spirit each day.

Monday - Love

Tuesday - Joy

Wednesday - Kindess

Thursday - Gentleness

Friday - Patience

Saturday - Goodness

Sunday - Self Control

THANK YOU

We hope you enjoyed this book, and we would love your feedback!

PLEASE LET US KNOW!

- Leave a review on Amazon
- Contact us directly

We look forward to hearing from you!
God bless you and your family!

Spirit of **TRUTH**

A podcast by Melissa Collins

Made in the USA
Columbia, SC
29 July 2024